Tickets for a Prayer Wheel

TICKETS
FOR A
PRAYER WHEEL

POEMS BY ANNIE DILLARD

PERENNIAL LIBRARY

Harper & Row, Publishers
New York, Cambridge, Philadelphia, San Francisco
London, Mexico City, São Paulo, Singapore, Sydney

ACKNOWLEDGMENTS

The American Scholar: "The Man Who Wishes to Feed on Mahogany"; *The Atlantic:* "Feast Days: Christmas"; *Carolina Quarterly:* "The Dominion of Trees," "After Noon"; *Contempora:* "Farmer's Daughter," "Tying His Tie and Whistling a Tune, Zimmer Strikes a Nostalgic Note and Invents his Past"; *The Hollins Critic:* "Christmas"; *Mill Mountain Review:* "Bivouac," "Some Questions and Answers about Natural History"; *Monmouth Review:* "My Camel"; *New Orleans Review:* "The Boston Poems of H* Ch* M*nh," © 1970 by Loyola University, New Orleans (reprinted by permission of the *New Orleans Review*); *New York Quarterly:* "Eleanor at the Office"; *Southern Poetry Review:* "Arches and Shadows"; *Transatlantic Review:* "Overlooking Glastonbury." I am also indebted to Edwin Way Teale, whose *The American Seasons* I quote in "Feast Days."

A hardcover edition of this book was published by University of Missouri Press. It is here reprinted by arrangement with the author.

First PERENNIAL LIBRARY edition published 1986.

Library of Congress Cataloging-in-Publication Data

Dillard, Annie.
   Tickets for a prayer wheel.

   Includes bibliographical references.
   "PL/7014."
   I. Title.
[PS3554.I398T5   1986]   811'.54   85-45629
ISBN 0-06-097014-6 (pbk.)

86   87   88   89   90   MPC   10   9   8   7   6   5   4   3

FOR RICHARD

Contents

I would be thought, being wholly thought. Amen.

I would be washed, and I would wash. Amen.

Grace danceth. *I would pipe, dance ye all.*

I would mourn: lament ye all. Amen.

—Apocryphal Acts of St. John

Tickets for a Prayer Wheel

Feast Days

Thanksgiving–Christmas

I

Three things are too wonderful for me;
    four I do not understand:
the way of an eagle in the sky,
    the way of a serpent on a rock,
the way of a ship on the high seas,
    and the way of a man with a maiden.
—Proverbs

Today I saw a wood duck
in Tinker Creek.
In the fall flood, look
what the creek floats down:
once I glimpsed
round the edge of a bank
a troupe of actors
rained in from Kansas,
dressed for comedy.
The flood left a candelabrum
on the lawn.
With a ten-foot hook
we fished from the creek
a bunch of bananas, a zither,
a casket of antique coins.

Or,
in the creek I found a log,
a tree trunk rotted halfway open.
Lord, lover, listen:
        I remember kissing on the stair
        dancing in the kitchen—
I crumbled the wet wood away.
Inside the tree a row of cells had grown,
sealed chambers, smooth, elongate.
I slit one open, found a book

hand-bound in yellow thread:
a child's book of wildflowers
sketched in ink
and washed with watercolors.
    Come take a walk, you said.
    And if I reached out
    my hand could feel your shoulders move,
    thin, under your shirt.
What newness, what surprises!
Once I dug a hole to plant a pine
and found a ruby growing on a stone.

One thing we've got plenty of
here on the continents
is soil. Out of the soil
the plants are taking substance, edges,
like a tomato moving on its stake,
ten pounds of tomatoes, and the ground
blowing them up like balloons.
We walk on the soil
here on the continents
among the plants, and eat.

Thanksgiving: the men
are watching the game.
I wash, and dry, and dream.
I dream of a firelit room,
a tipi of eighteen buffalo hides,
of skins on the floor
and smoke curling up
the bark of the trunk of the lightwood lodgepole pine.

The Mandans in North Dakota
along the Missouri, prayed,
Go, flying birds, to the southern horizon,
to the old woman who never dies.
Return at the end of winter.
Carry sunshine, carry water
on your broad backs.

And in your beaks,
and in your beaks,
bring her blessing like a berry
to the crops you symbolize—
"The wild goose to the maize,
the wild duck to the beans,
the wild swan to the gourds."

Thanksgiving, creation:
outside the great American forest
is heaving up leaves and wood from the ground.
Inside I stand at the window, god,
with your name wrapped round my throat like a scarf.

Today I've been naming
the plants of the southern forest:
arrowwood, witherod,
hobblebush, nannyberry,
and the loblolly, longleaf
and shortleaf pine.

Lean through the willow, look
upstream, and see what's floating down!
I see camels swimming
with long-lash, golden eyes.
I see trunks and telescopes floating,
a canopied barge with silk scarves flying,
a peacock on each post,
and three crowned kings inside.
Caspar, Melchior, Balthazar,
I suspect you're on to something.

You tell me your dream
and I'll tell you mine.

I dreamed I woke in a garden.
Everywhere trees were growing;
everywhere flowers were growing,
and otters played in the stream, and grew.
Fruit hung down.

An egg at my feet
cracked, opened up,
and you stepped out,
perfect, intricate lover.

II

Woman, why weepest thou?
Whom seekest thou?
—John

December, and all its dark rains.
The apples in the cellar
are black, and dying inside their skins.
They pray all night in their bins,
but nobody listens;
they will be neither food nor trees.
Outside in the city
the cop wants to dig out his earmuffs,
the orange ones,
and if it were snowing he might,
but it's only rain.

God send us the springtime lamb
minted and tied in thyme
and call us home, and bid us eat
and praise your name.

God am I smug when they talk about Belsen—
I've never killed anyone in my life!
I simply betray:

let the phone ring,
seal a typed letter,
say to the girl in the courtyard,
"I never saw him before in my life,"
call a cab, pull on gloves,
and leave. And leave you,
and leave you with the bill.

"Home," I say to the cabby,
"home, driver, to Tinker Creek.

It's in Virginia."
And he says, "Sorry, honey,
you can't get there from here."
"Then driver, please," I say,
"put me to bed."

Take a hot bath; take
a cold shower.
In your mouth stick
a silver spoon
so you don't crack.

Today you hurt your hand
on the fireplace.
Tonight a Chinook
rose up from the south.
And my mouth
stuck shut,
my belly shook,
my eyes blinked hot,
and I went to the window.

There, stalking the lawn,
white tipis, wraith-like, ranged.
A smell of blood burned up.
The moon bruised down.
Antlers hung in the trees.
A thousand tipi doors lashed back,
void, like riven graves.

And in the creek,
in Tinker Creek,
a sky-high blackened hull rose up,
a red-stacked ocean liner, sailing upstream.

They're on the roof,
naked, but I hear them.
I remember reading
in my room, just reading,
and shutting the book,
and looking up,

and missing you, missing you,
and reading the paper again.
There's no freedom in it
or in fear:
my heart's not mine.
Once I went to the door,
and an old black woman was there,
in a clown suit
and a clown's peaked hat,
and she carried a brown cloth bag.
Once an ape trailed through the hall
in my nightgown.
Once I surprised in the bathroom
the last of the Inca kings,
tall Atahualpa,
in his hand-stitched bat-skin robe.

"Don't worry," I said.
"It's all right," I said,
and ducked.

Oh, I've been here and there
around the heart—
a few night spots, really,
the kind that call themselves "Rathskellers,"
dim-lit, always changing hands,
and frequented on Sundays.
By the regulars:
mother in mink on the bar,
father looking up the grate to the sidewalk,
babies battling on the floor,
some sort of red-eyed monk
with a black-eyed mynah bird,
a clown (that clown!)—
and you,
variously:
weeping at the piano,
eating fly-blown meat with a spoon,
swirling a beer, and saying,

"Marry me"; or
"I read your letter
(diary, palm)"; or
"You don't understand."
And then always,
"Good-bye"
(So long, Take care)—
remember?
And then I leave.
I'm always the one who leaves.

God send us the springtime lamb
minted and tied in thyme
and call us home, and bid us eat
and praise your name.

III

And the captain of the Lord's host
said unto Joshua, Loose thy shoe
from off thy foot; for the place
whereon thou standest is holy.
—Joshua

I love with my hand, not my heart.
When I draw your face,
my fingers trace your lips.
Crossing a page, my hand keeps
contours; I know that art
is edges.
I touch when I type.
With every finger's tip
I travel the weave of the given.
Hand me a pencil,
cut off my head,
and I will draw you heaven.

Thank you, Squanto,
for the tip.
I knew something smelled funny in Iowa:
all that haddock, under the corn.

Mound-builders,
basketmakers,
cliff-dwellers—
all are gone to the sandhills.
Remember Sand Creek!
Remember Wounded Knee!
Remember how to fish?
You may have my salmon rights
to Tinker Creek.
Just keep off the roof;
it's coming up Christmas.

Under the water the wood duck
feels with his foot in the creek.

By day I cook, and we eat.
At night your hand curls over my head,
curls into my hair as you sleep.
Hands curl up
like leaves. My hand curls up
from the fire to the tipi top
and out.
My hand curls down
the wood duck's throat.
In the curl of my hand I hold corn.

I kick through a forest of hands
by Tinker Creek. The sassafras hands
wear mittens; the tulip tree hands
demand money; "Wait!" cry the fraying hands
of a frivolous silver maple,
"I love you!"
A cottonwood hand floats down the creek
on its back, like Ophelia.

And deep on the banks of the creek
some hands uncurl;
some hands unleaf, and damply become
rich water,
wild and bitter perfume,
and loam, where bluets will bloom.

So your hand, asleep in my hair,
takes root, and flowers there.

Let me mention
one or two things about Christmas.
Of course you've all heard
that the animals talk
at midnight:
a particular elk, for instance,
kneeling at night to drink,
leaning tall to pull leaves
with his soft lips,
says, alleluia.

That the soil and fresh-water lakes
also rejoice,
as do products
such as sweaters
(nor are plastics excluded
from grace),
is less well known.
Further:
the reason
for some silly-looking fishes,
for the bizarre mating
of certain adult insects,
or the sprouting, say,
in a snow tire
of a Rocky Mountain grass,
is that the universal
loves the particular,
that freedom loves to live
and live fleshed full,
intricate,
and in detail.

God empties himself
into the earth like a cloud.
God takes the substance, contours
of a man, and keeps them,

dying, rising, walking,
and still walking
wherever there is motion.

At night in the ocean
the sponges are secretly building;
by day in a pharmacy drawer
capsules stir in their jars.
Once, on the Musselshell,
I regenerated an arm!
Shake hands. When I stand
the blood runs up.
On what bright wind
did god walk down?
Swaying under the snow,
reeling minutely,
revels the star-moss,
pleased.

And to all you children out there with Easter bunnies
I would like to say this:
If they are chocolate, eat them.
If they are living, tuck them in your shirt.
There's always unseasonable weather.
Hose down the hutches.
For a special treat
to brighten up their winter
offer the early shoots of the wild American orchid,
the lady's-tresses,
in either of three varieties:
the slender, the hooded, or the nodding.

I

Beauty beyond thought everywhere, beneath,
above, made and being made forever.
—John Muir

The Man Who Wishes to Feed on Mahogany

Chesterton tells us that if someone wished to feed exclu-
sively on mahogany, poetry would not be able to express
this. Instead, if a man happens to love and not be loved in
return, or if he mourns the absence or loss of someone, then
poetry is able to express these feelings precisely because
they are commonplace.
—Borges, interview in *Encounter*, April, 1969

Not the man who wishes to feed on mahogany
and who happens to love and not be loved in return;
not mourning in autumn the absence or loss of someone,
remembering how, in a yellow dress, she leaned
light-shouldered, lanky, over a platter of pears—
no; no tricks. Just the man and his wish, alone.

That there should be mahogany, real, in the world,
instead of no mahogany, rings in his mind
like a gong—that in humid Haitian forests are trees,
hard trees, not holes in air, not nothing, no Haiti,
no zone for trees nor time for wood to grow:
reality rounds his mind like rings in a tree.

Love is the factor, love is the type, and the poem.
Is love a trick, to make him commonplace?
He wishes, cool in his windy rooms. He thinks:
of all earth's shapes, her coils, rays and nets,
mahogany I love, this sunburnt red,
this close-grained, scented slab, my fellow creature.

He knows he can't feed on the wood he loves, and he won't.
But desire walks on lean legs down halls of his sleep,
desire to drink and sup at mahogany's mass.
His wishes weight his belly. Love holds him here,
love nails him to the world, this windy wood,
as to a cross. Oh, this lanky, sunburnt cross!

Is he sympathetic? Do you care?
And you, sir: perhaps you wish to feed
on your bright-eyed daughter, on your baseball glove,

on your outboard motor's pattern in the water.
Some love weights your walking in the world;
some love molds you heavier than air.

Look at the world, where vegetation spreads
and peoples air with weights of green desire.
Crosses grow as trees and grasses everywhere,
writing in wood and leaf and flower and spore,
marking the map, "Some man loved here;
and one loved something here; and here; and here."

Tying His Tie and Whistling a Tune, Zimmer Strikes a Nostalgic Note and Invents His Past

The room where ladies move
their bosoms to the bath;

the room of doors, a wall
of closets like a train,
the footstool on the floor
where Mother fell;

the room where you burn yourself;
the beer-making room;
the room of wool.

The room of finches—
if you knock, they fly.

I remember the room of the poet,
with bold roll moldings in the beams,
with an antique clock
tricked out in silk
and twin glass doors to the park.

Some Questions and Answers about Natural History

Some Questions with Answers

Question: What do fish do
when floods come over—
kiss onto a tree root and squeeze?

Answer: There are no
fish in our rivers and streams.
The fauna you see
were bank and basement dwellers.
Fresh-water fish
all live in the ocean;
salt-water fish fall as rain.

Question: What causes
the wind? Why do I feel some way
in wind?

Answer: Trees
fan the wind as they sway.
Bushes help.
Your heart fills up.

Question: What color are fish?

Answer: No one has ever seen fish.
Fish secrete highly reflective compounds
that act as a skin of mirror.
It is thought that fishes' sides
are painted in landscapes,
mountainous.

Question: Clouds?

Answer: Mare's-tails, nocti-
luminescent, camel—signs of
storm, fresh air,

a heartbreaking journey.
Aurora australis
not a cloud.
Caused by hidden moon's glare
on the highest ice
reflected on sheer atomic curtains,
otherwise invisible.
Did you think it was a cloud?

Some Questions Without Answers

Question: Why do fireflies,
the spring ones, always say " **J** "?
Who is this **J**? Where should I go?

Question: Can birds move eggs?
Will you come
if I walk to the rivertree
and back? The skin on your eyelids
is one cell deep.

Some Answers Without Questions

Answer: Drawn by your sweet breath.
Sing or call
by the edge of the water at night.
Aim between the shoulders.

Answer: Contrary to common opinion,
most birds are blind.
Their highly developed sense of touch,
however, is pulled, so to speak,
like a stream.
Possibilities include: Polaris,
wistfulness, sudden memories,
ionization, and neap tides
such as are found
here, on the Bay of Fundy,
and elsewhere.

The Clearing

They came to the forest and made a clearing,
blasted the stumps, split the wood,
and built the woodshed.
                          Too tired
to build the house, they bought a roller,
white paint, some asphalt,
and made a tennis court in the clearing.

They forgot the fence. They played tennis
that summer till all the balls were lost
in the forest;
                   and when the woodshed
caught fire, it was almost as pretty
as the blaze the sparkler factory made
when it burned outside of Wheeling, West Virginia.

An Epistemology of Planets

Mercury

A brook runs on all night;
a book, shut,
still tells itself a story.
So you, out of thought,
you, forgotten Mercury,
still spin and spend the circles of your fury.

Venus

Evenings, after I've eaten
dessert, you rise, you wear
your barest, shining skin.

Later, mornings, you up
and do it again.

Do you think I've forgotten so soon?

Earth

Planets, alone, and grieving,
look who you're running with:
look at our baby-blue planet the earth
and all of the people, waving.

Mars

Mars keeps its dignity,
its networks of cool.
Certain photographs reveal
an air of longing, still.

Jupiter

Swings, spattered
by shadows of Jovian moons:
Io, Europa, Callisto,

the giant, Ganymede.
Companionable, each

nonetheless keeps

the perfected arc of his distance.

Saturn

It is to you I come in my dream,
you, dancing alone in the dark, light-heart,
asleep inside your spinning hat!

Uranus

Uranus, cold face,
old rock and ice,
remembers a song
and sings it once
round the dark, twice.

Neptune

Banished, Neptune,
luminous, green,
sleeps, and dreams of the sun.
Awake, he holds her round
as tight as he can.

Pluto

Spends twenty years
wandering in Cancer,
that old celestial
crab. Takes years to touch
carapace, jointed foot
on jointed leg; nudges
mandibles, roving, awed,
in every season.
Getting to know
you, still, I find you clear-eyed,
cloistered, clawed.

Tan from the Sun

Q. Are you tan from the sun?
A. No, I'm Annie from earth.
—children's joke

Tan from the sun
is slick as a drop;
lollipop man, serene.

Halloo! he calls
down the hairless wind;
he has a little brain

like a ping-pong ball;
his fingernail
is lucid as the moon.

Annie from earth
has grit for teeth
and grasses on her chin.

Halloo! she calls;
her shoulder smells
of salt and fluid, stone.

Annie from earth
has twigs in her mouth;
she sleeps in a whitened gown

of bones like lace;
while Baby-face,
old Tan from the sun wakes on.

The Shape of the Air

Some Specifics

Cut a hole through the roof of your house
leading to your bedroom closet.
Close and caulk.
Stand on the roof,
pour plaster down
into your shoes,
around, through your shirts,
pants, bathrobe, hats, . . .
allow to dry.
Remove with hooks.
Split. Remove the clothes;
discard.
This is the shape of part of the air.

The shape of the air
around a sycamore
is shot with sparks,
elastic, slit with leaves.
The shape of the air
around a city
in cross section
is like a broken comb.

Look at the clouds
asleep on the gunwales,
like oars.
The shape of the air
over the mountain
is fringed as a fin.
Shearwaters stitch and rend:
pickerel, over the side.

The air folds around
a muskrat out on a bank.

The air slides a slipper,
cool, under his lifted foot.
He dives. Air closes
the space where he stood.
Do you think
fish out of water leave holes?

He swims; his nose is the merest pit.
There's a bow-wave on the water,
and the air over the river,
tremulous, fans at the keel like a shell.

Everywhere air over a river
stays, pressing just so on the reeds,
hovers, while water
under its belly slides down.

With time, money, effort,
and, above all, the cooperation
of her citizens,
we could determine
the shape of the air
around the United States of America.

The Influence of Wind

The wind can't change
the shape of the air,
except as it curls the hemlock's back
and shoots the air scratched
out to lee,
where it spreads on the lawn.
The wind
slashes a slit up the air
where it splits down a totem-pole
eagle's beak. Then too,
there's a way
an offshore wind
sticks in the craw of a wave.

The Girl in the Birchbark Canoe

The girl in the birchbark canoe
gazes ahead.
Her back is straight; her fingers
twist in her lap; her face
pales; her lips part.
Her look drifts down
the dry, cavernous room,
the dark one,
the Hall of the Americas.

The girl
climbed in the museum's birchbark canoe
in April, and has lived there since.
Crowds came, and thinned.
Her visitors leave food.

She speaks:
what happens to muskrats
when rivers freeze over?
She sleeps
under a split ash thwart in the stern.

The Shape of the Air
Around the Girl in the Birchbark Canoe

Willow and skins
make a calm-water bullboat;
it raises
a bowlful of air from the floor.
There's a thorn
of tipi up the air, a splinter
of kayak. The top of the air
loops like an acrobat round the rough
sides of a forty-man dugout
hung from the roof.

The keel of the birchbark canoe
is pitched with resin;
the keel of the museum's air still smells
of the volatile oils of pine.
The air round the birchbark canoe
catches in curves,
like ice in tongs.

The shape of the air
round the girl in the birchbark canoe
is a spoon through the part in her lips.
Air makes inlets up her fingers,
grooves, transparent.

When she moves,
the air sways and fills.
Air cups at her eyes.
Warm slabs of air
from her shoulders rise,
spread to the plaster dome.
Broadside,
concentric arcs of air
swell in a cone
of her mother,
her father,
calling out
across wild white water.

Day at the Office

Typewriter keys think of themselves
as a unit, like volvox, or moss.
But the space bar,
prone, is our darling.

Nothing is plotting.
The wastebasket is not secretive;
it completes. It extols.
Only the curtains still keep
their languorous, droll counsel.

The envelope drawer is perhaps
the room's most innocent feature,
unfaltering. Restless, the vitreous
ashtrays swarm, ashtrays swarm.

The thermostat—to take
an example—the thermostat
is a child merely, uncomprehending.
Avuncular, swivel chairs
peer and indulge.

Ho, under the water cooler,
by the dusty part of the wall,
there's an earring, dropped, made from a shell.

II

Behold, the days come, saith the Lord
God, that I will send a famine in the land,
not a famine of bread, nor a thirst for
water, but of hearing the words of the Lord:
And they shall wander from sea to sea,
and from the north even to the east, they
shall run to and fro to seek the word of the
Lord, and shall not find it.
—Amos

Death-runes, death-rumours, ruins and rains
of death.
—John Cowper Powys

Bivouac

I

The she-wolf whelps in thunder.
The new-born prophet licks his palms
to clean his face like a cat.
You wake on the shore, weeping,
biting your own salt knee.

> You remember, don't you?
> You remember the sea,
> the deep sea, the pressure,
> and the pebbled shallows
> where the nurse sharks wait
> to heave you toward the light. . . .

You wake on the shore,
sand and gravel under your back,
wrack and sand in your hair.
Blink, and the light gives way
to the fixed and waterless stars.

You wake. The ocean
is furling its green tons down.
Volcano weather.
The sharp-shinned hawk
cleaves with intricate strain
to the skin of air rivers rising,
spreading, peeling half over
and off to the side like a leaf.

This is the mainland,
this heaping of stones and the pines.
And the barnacles—
remember?—
when the water came over,
you waved your feathery arms.

The sky never ceases to widen,
hollow, over your head.
You can fashion
a fish-life here on the coast,
willow-strip, driftwood
and dugout, or go in
to a land already planted.

    You remember, don't you?
    You remember the forest,
    the deep jungle, the tree ferns,
    the club mosses, the green air;
    turning a golden eye to watch
    the lizards still on the stones. . . .

There's forest inside, straight wood,
a mud clearing, and a man
on his knees shaking feathers,
owl feathers, owl tongues, twisted
in sinew and thong.

And there's desert inside,
caves and a woman
splitting her lips with a thorn.
This is your son, and your daughter.

    You remember, don't you?
    You remember the plains,
    the wind, the hot grass,
    hefting a gritty rock
    to split thick bones and suck
    the bloody grease. . . .

Follow the rivers, look for a pass,
or follow the ridges, rise.
There are no eyes on you.
You were kindled from a clot
and washed on the beach like a conch
from one more witless wave.

II

You have never been so tired.

The wooded ridges roll under the sun
like water, and none of the mountains home,
and all of the mountains bivouac,
campaigner; lean-to, hoe-down, shack-up: run.

III

A baby is a pucker
of the earth's thin skin;
he swells, circles, and lays him down.

The lakes fill, the ice rolls back,
(the ice rolls up!) the ice rolls back,
the skin wrinkles and splits—
fishes, grass—the skin
bunches and smooths.

You die, you die.
First you go wet
and then you go dry.

This is the end,
the dry channel,
the splintered sluice,
where you slake your thirst on chert.
There's a spread to the light
and a rising, a way
that even the air is a cobra;
and at night
the rock moon and the desert rock
bat the dead light back
and forth till it snaps.

You sleep
under a ledge away from the river bed;

you wake
to the sun looming low like the mouth
of a tunnel to hell.
A scale-legged bird is eating a snake.
Dig for mice. Smell
your shoulder. There's been
flash-flood, dust-storm,
rivers run in and moved out
like haunts, and still those two round lights,
the fire-light and the ash;
and still you wake, you wake a million days,
and walk.

Oh yes,
it's a hard slide,
it's a rough winter,
what with the sharp gravel
and acid salts in the sand.
You're softshell and peeled,
with nothing to keep out the wind—
the williwaw, cheechako—
that splits the cell and drains it dry as ash.

IV

You have walked beyond
the highest tide and seen
how, where birds have landed,
walked, and flown,
their tracks begin in sand,
and go, and suddenly end.
Our tracks do that, but we go down.

Where have we been,
and why do we go down?
At night your best-loved dead appear
back, and start their stare.

You wake; you greet them;
you wake again; the dead still steer
their sleeping course,
their sleeping heels in the air.

Hold fast.
Duck.
There's a flat-out, flinging way
the clouds begin their dive,
there's a scurf of earth and air
so thin
you'd step clear through
or blow clean off.

> You remember it all:
> how you lungless lay in slime,
> how you shied across the plain
> on your sharp split hoof,
> the mist, the sip of ozone on the tongue. . . .

You wake. This is the mainland.
Here you must look
at each thing with the elephant eye:
greeting it now for the first time,
and bidding, forever, good-bye.

Ease her when she pitches.
Keep your tinder dry.

Arches and Shadows

He proposed to me on the Ferris wheel—
I nearly fell off!—and once we dived
off the board holding hands, I remember,
though not very clearly. O it may not have been
croquet on the lawn and twenty for dinner,
but we had our times, sir, and I had mine,
awaiting election returns with the old crowd
before I left. In Trieste I said Promise
you'll always love me, I actually said that,
and at the fair in Brussels I made
an extremely witty remark. A white puppy
followed me all one afternoon, all
around the race track. He promised;
he said we would live in a houseboat—
raise ponies—sell apples—dry flowers—
all this in a peat-fire pub on Exmoor;
I was sunburned all over, even my hands.
Now in November when the cat wants out early,
it's your face I see in the folds of my dress on the chair.
I'll meet you in March in Alberta;
today I sewed a pleat and cut a lemon in your name,
thinking: then I will travel the Great Northern Railways
and we can talk things over, sitting down.

The Boston Poems of H* Ch* M*nh

Before World War I, under his real name, Nguyen
That Thanh, he [Ho Chi Minh] shipped around the
world as a cabin boy on the French liner, D'Artagnan.
During this period, he claims to have worked as a
waiter in Boston, a dishwasher in New York and London,
a photo retoucher in Paris.
—Parade, *February 12, 1967*

I

On the ocean, what may we observe?
I may observe nothing on the ocean
for La Comtesse must be served.
Down below the water line
La Comtesse is waiting.
I will give her old wine,
Rhine wine, gladly,
knowing my duty, understanding
women, and French.

II

If I weep for Annam
it is only because
La Comtesse has an odor;
it is only because this morning
the Indian Ocean soaked through my shoes
and I thought I stood in Annam,
amidst irrigation.

III

Water follows me to London.
In Annam, water is precious
except when it rains;
on the ocean, there is a surfeit;
here I have dishpan hands.
The ladies are gay in Boston,
in New York, in London,
and their liveries elegant.

Crêpe de Chine roses
blossom in their hats,
and the morsels they leave
on their plates are tasty.
My delicate liver accustoms itself
to fat meat;
who shall my sisters marry
among the gentle men of Annam?

IV

Léon Daudet is in Paris
advocating return to the monarchy.
The sage has an old face, a hairy face,
and I erase its wrinkles—
I, Nguyen That Thanh, photo-retoucher,
son of Annam.

V

I went to a seer in Paris
who shook her head and whispered,
"It's rough days ahead in Bosnia,
a most inauspicious season."
"What of my sisters?" I asked her,
"What of Annam?" "I must advise
against a trip to Bosnia
at this time." It is June in Paris,
rainy season in Annam. I will not
seek her out again.

VI

At nineteen I traveled south
to Cochin China from Faifoh
and left the silver rice-fields of Annam.
I have known London, Dresden,
Alsace-Lorraine. Now I am almost eighty;
my eyes water; my enemies strengthen
in the fields and here at home.

Eleanor at the Office

Eleanor at the water cooler,
weeping, laps cold water.

Everyone wishes she felt better.

Stephen always watches you;
Marian watches you, beloved;
William watches you always.

You are young!
You should not ever cry!
You dropped your earring:

a dropped earring behind the water cooler,
a dropped earring on oak flooring;
a shell on your left ear
(Eleanor, marry me),
and your right ear's bare.

Farmer's Daughter

There's always unseasonable weather.
Remember the flood that killed father:
when the water went down, the chickens
lay muddy and drowned. Oh we watch
the weather here on earth; we don't forget
the winter days when girls wear cotton dresses,
the Aprils when the bushes sag with snow.
> We were cutting the apple trees back
> when he said, "Look, it's snowing";
> but I'd seen a winter of snow
> and knew that more were coming.
Still, what do we know of a season?
Only father could say
when the rain would stop at the mountain
or ruin the hay. I'd try to watch
the hawks or lick a finger,
and the crops were still a failure;
there was frost all over the valley,
south as far as Twin Falls.
> He kissed me when shadows were long
> on the path to the orchard; he promised
> to meet me again when the apples were in;
now when the wind parts the curtains,
now in the city when the cat won't come,
I sleep with only one eye shut,
keeping a weather eye out.

The Dominion of Trees

For the Robinsons

I

Trees preserve dominion,
put competition
in the shade. We eat
our fruit, slice
our meat in this green shade.
Listen,
under the arches of your bare feet
where you run, Teresa,
white roots suck up their watery salts.

II

Here ground speaks
its one word: tree.
No handle hits ax
more square, more fixed
than these trunks grow,
these speeches
of rock rise up.
But look,
loose at the top,
sun and soil have their leafy say.

III

Falling from trees,
children accelerate
thirty-two feet
per second, per second.
Lie in the dark,
shine a lantern up—
color! leaves still green.

Under your back,
ground water walks
a mile a year.

IV

If Monica fell in the woods
and nobody heard,
someone would run and call
Monica, Monica!
even under the crowfeather leaves
when the sun was gone.

V

Deciduous trees
have dominion.
But look on bark;
molds make fruiting bodies
out of air. Winner
take all. Grab
a handle. Earth
rolls down like dolphins dive,
headlong to dark.

VI

Little-flesh,
you run aimless around
on the blade of an ax,
eating tomatoes. Trees
have dominion.
                    We play
at their feet; we work
up a run, under trees.

After Noon

Winter: bright babies,
where are your holes-in-one now
that the windmill is still,
that the barn door is still,
that the fountain is still
on the miniature golf course?

Mother, I want to go home.
I know I shall always love her,
I shall never forget her that summer—
was it Rome, Mother do you remember?
The coat she was wearing was green,
and her shoes had such odd little buckles.

Overhead glare flattens the grass—
our wintery, raggedy home.
It was colorful there by the lamplight,
wasn't it, Mother, and gay?
It must have been gay, I remember
the comic strips spread on the floor.

Overlooking Glastonbury

Und die Hörner des Sommers verstummten
—Georg Heym

Now the horns of summer fall silent
in the swaying meadows of rain.
Wild, this house and garden
shrink beneath swirling skies.

There is a stake
through the statue's marble heart,
and her head snaps off,
laughing. The water cools,
the wicker basket
fills with dolls,
a knife waits in the goblet
on your white,
your wafer-white plate,
and look: two swans
curl feathered necks
in the lake,
the black lake,
love it is, or lust,
lust, and the clatter of bells.

Words to an Organ Grinder's Music

Wake me, Weston, and say
when the sun goes down
that you love me, and stay
at the foot of my bed till morning.

All I want's a little comfort!

And a ten-dollar bill in my shoe,
a dab of Drambuie with coffee,
and you, old early riser, old
Druid, old lounge-lizard you.

About Eskimos

Eskimos, toothless,
on the move, practice
cruelty to animals;

mend traces; build
ice houses, warm,
where warm air rises.

On the move, it is hard.
Many Eskimos starve.
Those who live, move.

On clear days, large mammals
on the move, leave trails
floating, of mammal breath.

Watch the trails, watch
your step. Chew, if you must,
quietly. You can catch

an Eskimo: File your teeth.
Mark his path. If you see
an igloo, hold your breath.

III

I think I have told you, but if I have not,
you must have understood, that a man who has
a vision is not able to use the power of it
until after he has performed the vision
on earth for the people to see.
—Black Elk

With all your science can you tell how it is,
and whence it is, that light comes into
the soul?
—Henry David Thoreau

God

Numbers from one to ten, however, are called
"God." In other words, counting to ten you would
say, "God, God, God, God, God, God, God, God, God,
God." It is possible to distinguish among these
numbers by the tone in which each is pronounced.
"God," for example, corresponding to our "five,"
is pitched relatively high on the musical scale,
and accordingly sounds an inquisitive, even plaintive,
note. It is in sharp contrast to the number corre-
sponding to our "ten," which has a slightly accented,
basso finality, thus: "God."

My Camel

A dialogue of self and soul

I snared him with a jackknife
and a four-foot length of gut
before his eyes were open,

or they were shut
against me. I cut
his tongue out; I seared

his bloody tongue-root shut.
Sun in your eye,
desert-heart:

do you even know I'm here?
I chew honey-locust pods;
I spit them down his throat.

For years I forget my camel.
He wanders, edged in light,
caked in grit, like a cloud.

Does he wander.
He scents up empty stream beds
with his nostril slits;

he kneels to sleep—
I watch him through the glass.
He's upside down

in the sky; behind
a pyramid, he splits
and crosses the lightest lakes

like Moses. Oh artful,
shaggy, folded:
I write the words

of your name on the lintel,
the gates of my house,
like a cloud,

on my hands' binding,
between my eyes,
so like a cloud.

Christmas

Trees that have loved
in silence, kiss,
crashing; the Douglas firs lean
low to the brittle embrace
of a lodgepole pine.

In cities at night
tin canisters eat
their cookies; the bed,
asleep, tossing,
brushes its curtain of bead.

My wristwatch grows
obscurely, sun-
flower big. Across
America, cameras gaze,
astonished, into the glass.

This is the hour
God loosens and empties.
Rushing, consciousness comes
unbidden, gasping,
and memory, wisdom, grace.

Birds come running;
the curtains moan.
Dolls in the hospital
with brains of coral
jerk, breathe and are born.

Puppy in Deep Snow

All of him goes under,
even tail, till, like a tiny whale,
he will surface anywhere
with a leap and then be lost
like a diving loon and then be tossed
like Saint Teresa making *grands jetés en l'air*.

Tickets for a Prayer Wheel

The son, a scholar, speaks:

Our family is looking
for someone who knows how to pray.
Ora pro nobis, pray for us now
and now.
            We sent
all our strong cousins out as runners. . . .

One of the cousins
brought back a doll
which he had purchased at great price.
The doll is dressed in feathers
and beads of mistletoe.
His head, according to our cousin,
is stuffed with millet seed;
on each seed is written,
in a tongue foreign to us,
"PRAY." We are uncertain
whether to shake the doll
like a rattle, or worship him.
We took turns wearing him
around our necks;
we may yet stew him
in a soup of herbed broths
and pass him round
and drink him up.

Whose prayers are good?
Whose prayers are good?

My book says,
"It is a characteristic practice
to write prayers on small leaves
which are then chewed
and fastened on the faces of the idols."

We have lost a taste for other foods.
I cannot cross a room without falling down.

My mother is piecing a cover
for Christ, if he should come.
She feeds all strangers; she saves
skins; her fingers pray over
wound wool on skeins.

Saint Irenaeus said
collective prayer
accompanied by fasting
could raise the dead.
Christ was unable to work
miracles, according to Luke,
in Nazareth,
where no one had faith.
Saint Irenaeus!
And the dead? And the dying?
I met him down the ruining stair,
wearing a necklace of macaws
threaded through the eyes;
I met him on the flat space
in the brain—
thin bones strewn
in a box, like lace.

Pray without ceasing.
Hoc licet orare,
quod licet desiderare.
Saint Thomas: we may pray
for all those things we are not
forbidden to want.
But Christ says needs:
your Father knows what you need
before you ask him;

your heavenly Father knows
that you need them all.

My sister,
who works well in small,
has made a device
to strap on her wrist.
A sensitive lever
that touches her pulse
flips open a door
to a circular well
in which is inscribed the word "GOD."
We hear her walking the halls
or shut in her windy rooms
clicking minutely her prayer.
And sometimes, look
how her heart beats hard:
GOD GOD GOD GOD GOD GOD GOD GOD GOD GOD. . . .

The Dominican,
Gregorio Lopez,
prayed continuously for three years,
"Thy will be done on earth
as it is in heaven."
If we all stop at once
will the arches collapse?
How were those three years?

There's someone else in the house;
I saw the edge
of his topcoat round the stair.
Mother went out to the kitchen for milk
and found a kettle of bones
boiling on the fire.
We smell
wind in our beds;
we sweep dead bees
and a deer leg from the fire.

Our astronomers have found and named
the two moons of Mars:
Phobos and Deimos,
dread and terror,
winding over the house.
What rood or aspergillum
banishes this brood?

We baited our hooks
with burnt pigeons,
with papers of prayer on a string
and pieces of fire that hissed in the river.
That night was clear; stars floated on water.
We baited our hooks
and cast them into the sky.

At dawn my father
drew in the line
and threw the doves to the dogs.
The papers of prayer were ruined,
the fires put out.
Reflections confuse our astronomers;
many doubt the accuracy of the casts.
Our gifts are rejected.
Our own people despise us.
Who will teach us to pray,
who will pray for us now?
Pascal:
"Every religion
which does not affirm that God is hidden
is not true."

*
*
*
*
*
*
*
*
*
*

The third horseman, and a voice:
"A quart of wheat for a denarius,
and three quarts of barley for a denarius;
but do not harm oil and wine!"
Fast days.

We feather our nests
with froth; the rivers roll,
the screens of mercy part. . . .
Needs, he says; knock; seek;
and still they die,
who do not wish to leave.
We must not need
life. "Not
as the world gives do I give to you."

My sister sleeps.
My father went away.
My mother serves a soup of smoke and snow.
How long has it been?
My diagrams
cancel each other out.
There is one prayer left:
"Teach us to pray."
Teach us to pray.

*
*
*
*
*
*
*
*
*

Later:
My mother lay
in a windless room
under blankets, on the floor.
The walls were cold,
the cloth hangings without color,
dry.
We live among the dead. . . .
By her bed
a wooden desk appeared,
stray, austere,
and on it four white cups—
earth, air, water, fire.

Many things are becoming
possible for us.
We are recalling
forgotten lore;
we are exploring
our own house and garden
like hard men charting
the Ultima Thule.

Martin Luther prayed for rain.
Under the hearth we dug down,
found rain water, salt,

and an old coin
printed with a gold cloud.
With ropes we drew up rocks
hung damp in sea thong,
living mussel.
Under the water grew eglantine,
standing either for Poetry
or the saying
"I wound to heal."

My father is back.
The house is a plain
the old man crazes through.
He has carved on his belly
and chest the Nicene Creed.
He rubs grit in
to raise the scars. . . .
VERY GOD OF VERY GOD
LIGHT OF LIGHT
GOD OF GOD

He wants to break his will
like a stick across the knee.
But God meets always
the prayer for faith.
Woe, my father cries one day,
and Mercy the next.
Once he snared a nun
and bid her beat him,
but she beat soft.
Rape? Imitation?
We kept her round the house
till she flew off.

Something is already here.
The prayer for faith
routs it out the air; or,

only faith can cry for itself
up the short, inspirited night
or down the drear day.

In Luke eleven
and again in Luke eighteen,
Christ demands
importunate prayer,
prayer that does not faint.
Fatigare deos,
wearing God out.
Is Christ as good as his word?

If God does not tire, still
we may tire of longing.
Pray this prayer:
receive our prayer.
Teach us to pray, teach us to pray, to pray, pray.

The river Chebar
flows to the sea;
the river Hiddekel
flows to the sea.
Maranatha, amen.
My sister stands like Archimedes,
drawing spirals in the sand.
When the wind comes
it washes her with spindrift;
water fills the spirals
where the sea grapes hatch.

Our cousin came
and called, "Hello, hello . . ."
"Ho!" we cried,
"If you are thirsty,
come down to the water;
ho, if you are hungry,
come and sit and eat."

At last we understood
he could not see
or hear us. We walked
in the sky; we were crossing
a wooden bridge across the sea.

                                        *
                                        *
                                        *
                                        *
                                        *
                                        *
                                        *
                                        *
                                        *
                                        *

You go down the hall
and open the door,
down the hall
and open the small door,
down the dark hall
and open the smaller door,
down the hall,
small as a wire,
bare, and the final door—
flies from the wall.

                                        *
                                        *
                                        *
                                        *
                                        *
                                        *
                                        *
                                        *
                                        *
                                        *

Now bright with flames,
growing more remote
up that holy wall,
and bring us, we thee, to its thrall.

We had a garden
by the river, in our yard with a stone wall.
My father liked often
to examine the picture,
the universe—he saw
the universe large overall
and clapped him in to itself,
to its ebon, annihilable thrall.
God held him close
and lighted for him
the distant, decaying stars,
God looped him,
in a sloping loop of stars.

He came back and asked
for a cup of cold water only.
He planted beans on the bookshelf,
they grew, and fed us
for a year. He said,
I cannot bind the chains of the Pleiades,
nor loose the cords of Orion.
The one and Holy God whatever can, alone,
whose hand is his face.
We pray at his command
a prayer of praise.

The presence of God
he pricked me up
and swung me like a bell.
I saw the tree
on fire, I sang
a hundred prayers of praise.

God in the house
teaching us to pray:
and the family crazed
and full of breath.

We nailed a picture
by the door, on the whitewashed wall.
My father leaned close
to examine the picture,
the universe—At once,
the universe rang its call
and clapped him in to itself,
to its ebon, unthinkable thrall.
God held him close
and lighted for him
the distant, dizzying stairs;
God looped him
in a sloping loop of stars.

He came back and asked
for a cup of cold water only.
He planted beans on the bookshelf;
they grew, and fed us
for a year. He said,
"I cannot bind the chains of the Pleiades,
nor loose the cords of Orion.
The one and holy God of heaven can, alone,
whose hand is his face.
We pray at his command
a prayer of praise."

The presence of God:
he picked me up
and swung me like a bell.
I saw the trees
on fire, I rang
a hundred prayers of praise.

I no longer believe
in divine playfulness.

I saw all the time of this planet
pulled like a scarf
through the sky.
Time, that lorn and furling
oriflamme . . .

Did God dilute
even his merest thought
and take a place in the scarf,
shrink and cross
to an olive continent
and eat our food at little tables for a time?
All those things
which were thought to be questions
are no longer important.
I breathe
an air like light;
I slough off questions
like a hundred suits of motley;
I wear a bright mandorla
like a gown.

We keep our paper money shut
in a box, for fear of fire.
Once, we opened the box
and Christ the lamb stepped out
and left his track of flame across the floor.

Why are we shown these things?
God teaches us to pray.

My sister
dreamed of a sculpture
showing the form of God.

He has no edges,
and the holes in him spin.
He alone is real,
and all things lie in him
as fossil shells
curl in solid shale.
My sister dreamed of God
who moves around
the spanding, spattered holes
of solar systems hollowed in his side.

I think that the dying
pray at the last
not "please"
but "thank you"
as a guest thanks his host at the door.
Falling from mountains
the people are crying
thank you,
thank you,
all down the air;
and the cold carriages
draw up for them on the rocks.

Fare away, fare away!

The Dominican
Gregorio Lopez
prayed on God's command.
A hand
raised my mother up,
and round her poured
a light like petalled water.
For thou only art holy,
thou only art the lord . . .
and we are drowned.